PRAISE FOR
MUSING ALOUD, ALLOWED

The poems in Sherna Spencer's *Musing Aloud, Allowed* reverberate with the tempo of the Caribbean, with the beat of life and love and with the sound of humanity, universal to us all.
>—**Rita Fidler Dorn**: poet, person, professor of English at Florida International University, Miami, FL Immediate Past president of South Florida Writers Association

The poems are quite thought and emotion, provoking. They are definitely nostalgic for those have a deep love for Jamaica and are now members of the Jamaican diaspora. She has also managed to capture the mood as well as the perils and challenges faced by the immigrant, especially those who are undocumented.
>—**Garth A. Rose**, PhD
>Editor, *National Weekly*, "The Most Widely Circulated Caribbean/American Newspaper in South Florida"

Ms. Spencer takes the reader through the eyes of an American Immigrant . . . she shares pains and discoveries of the journey. Each and every immigrant will find some of these words touching and revealing. There is love, there is loss, there is hope, there is a mirror for the souls.
>—**Martha E. Galindo** MA, CT.
>President and CEO, Galindo Publicidad Inc

Sherna's poems meld the sublime, the mundane and the subtle struggles within the human psyche, into a compelling narrative about the human journey. The beauty of her work is its capacity to make her personal truths, observations and inner sensibilities intimately yours.
>—**Philip Dickenson Peters**
> Author of *Caribbean Wow 2.0*, *Caribbean Zen* and *Manikato*

Musing Aloud, Allowed is a great body of work. Her poems are easily digested and satisfying to the intellect. They are a well needed statement that expresses the Caribbean culture, which Sherna delivers in a thought-provoking, funny and witty way; They leave you wanting more.
>—**Maxine J. Tulloch,** MBA
> Television Executive Producer & Host, Film Producer, Photographer, Public Speaker and Business Executive.

Sherna Spencer's *Musing Aloud, Allowed,* will have you doing just what the title suggests. The poems touches the reader with imagery and words that are both inspiring and satisfying! A must read on any given day!
>—**Dale Holness**
> Broward County Commissioner, State of Florida

MUSING ALOUD ALLOWED

Sherna Spencer

JALOUSIE

an Imprint of SGS Publishing, LLC

www.borntherelivehere.com

Musing Aloud, Allowed. Copyright © 2014, by Sherna G. Spencer. All rights reserved.

Except as permitted under the U.S. Copyright Act of 1976, no part of this publication may be reproduced, distributed, or transmitted in any form or by any means, or stored in a database or retrieval system, without the prior written permission of the publisher.

>Published by JALOUSIE
>an Imprint of SGS Publishing, LLC
>*www.borntherelivehere.com/musingaloud*

Musing Aloud, Allowed is a work of fiction. Names, characters, places, and incidents are the product of the author's imagination or are used fictionally. Any resemblance to actual events, locales, or persons, living or dead, is coincidental.

>ISBN: 978-0-9787613-0-1 (paperback)
>ISBN: 978-0-9787613-1-8 (ebook / Kindle & Mobi)
>ISBN: 978-0-9787613-2-5 (ePub)

Publisher's Cataloging-in-Publication data

Spencer, Sherna G.
>Musing Aloud, Allowed: collected poems, 2007–2014/Sherna Spencer
>p.cm
>Includes index
>ISBN 9780978761301
>1. Caribbean. 2. Poetry. Women writers. 3. Inspirational-Women. 4. Humor –Women. 5.Title-
>Library of Congress Control number 2013920665

First Edition: October 2014   SCANNABLE

Printed in the United States of America

Book design by DesignForBooks.com

Attention Corporations, Universities, Colleges and Professional Organizations. Quantity discounts are available on bulk purchases of this book for educational, gift purposes, or as premiums for increasing magazine subscriptions or renewals. Special books or book excerpts can also be created to fit specific needs. For information, please contact SGS Publishing, 4500 W. Oakland Park Boulevard, Ste 103, Fort Lauderdale, FL 33313: 954-714-8123. Sales@borntherelivehere.com

Dedication

*For Sunita and Sonnet, my reason for being.
For all of the immigrants who have
touched my life and in whose lives
I have made a difference
and for all the teachers who see themselves
in their students.*

ACKNOWLEDGEMENTS

The author wishes to express her gratitude to her editor, Rita F. Dorn. Thanks also, to Beresford Nicholson whose questions evoked more questions, causing more contemplation. Best to Danny Breakenridge for his support and encouragement. A Special thanks to Sandi Webster who told me to take my book out of the computer.

Contents

Table of Contents Story   xi
Preface   xiii

FOR THE NEW AMERICAN   1

YOU are America   3
The Reunited   5
The Undocumented   7

JAMAICA CALLING

How to Listen to Reggae (Vibing on Bob)   11
Jamaica Goodbye   13

HUMOR FOR ANY AGE AND STAGE   19

Children are Like Sweets   21
How to Take Your Medicine   23
Sir Pride   25

INSPIRATIONAL   29

Fight Right   31
Little Treasures   33
Love   35
Me Hiding   38
Rise to the Beat   39
Sow Stones, Reap Daffodils?   40

Musing Aloud, Allowed

Taboo, Thank You   42
Wind Catcher   43

SOCIAL COMMENTARY   45

A Word to the Faithful   47
Designed for Extinction   48
Divide and Conquer   49
Fringe Rule   55
Letter to the Upsetters   59
More Laws, Less Happiness   61
News   63
OxyMoron   64
Politricks = Politics   65
The Devil is in the Details   66
The Skin I'm In   69
Travel Ban   72

MUSING ALOUD   75

Call to Order   77
Creative Writing 101   79
Crosses to Bear   81
Father's Day is Every Day   82
Genius   84
Gifting   85
I am Willing   87
More Than Just a Number   88
Small Talk Just Got Smaller   90
Snap, Pop and Pour   92
The Point of Ranting   93
Tone Deaf   95

Table of Contents Story

Ranting Genius with Crosses to Bear, listening to Reggae, Politics and Politricks; writing 101 Creative Letters to the Upsetters, calling them oxyMORONS—on behalf of the Undocumented. I don't want to be rude and say, A Call to Order, because the response will be, you Devil you have too many Details, too many Laws, less Happiness, trying to Divide and Conquer with Fringe Rules and Travel Bans. My response would be—I am Willing, I know you are More than Just a Number, let's just get to the point, short clear sentences—Small Talk. I'll arrange an event where we can Snap, Pop and Pour and I'll do a lot of Gifting. I'll also stop pretending to be Tone Deaf. Let's bury the hatchet. Today is Father's Day and I've got great News, the Taboo is off. That's what happens when you're Faithful, Sir. When you Sow the Right Stones, you Reap Daffodils, you Rise to the Beat. It is designed that way. So come out of Hiding, Take Your Medicine, don't Fight, its all done because of Love. We want to Treasure you. You want to say Goodbye to Jamaica? Fly away then, ride the Wind. You are America too. You can reunite with your loved ones there, after all, they are your sKIN.

Preface

When I looked inside and saw this title	I thought:
Jamaica Goodbye	Who's leaving?
YOU are America	YOU who?
Sir Pride	Why not Mistress Pride?
Letter to the Upsetters (The Banned Books Crusaders)	Wow . . . have to read this!
Love	A Dear John/Jane or Tina Turner?
Taboo, Thank You	Is'nt that a restaurant?
How to Take Your Medicine	Not with a glass of water?
How to Listen to Reggae (Vibing on Bob)	I'm all ears and hips!

For the New American

YOU are America

YOU are America
Your blood, sweat and tears

You are the Silicon in the Valley
the bits in the Wall that made the Street,
the China in the American town
and the story that makes Hollywood the blockbuster
You are the Apple that makes New York big.

Your blood runs deep in the New York subways
it stands tall in the turrets of the San Francisco Bay Bridge
it dampens the ground on the farms and in the orchards
and creates the vines in the valley of the wine.

Your sweat scents the hills in the spring
touring on the backs of the bees pollinating.
Your skin is kissed by the summer
its luster coats your pores in autumn and
in winter, seeping into the socks,
the leather and the rubber,
as you go from dawn till dusk
and into the midnight shift.

Your tears dampen the sheets and the pillowcases you fold
they follow you through the residences with
five, four and even three stars.
They keep you company as doors swish inward and
outward in the emergency rooms,
at airports and seaports,
where you stuff the letter with your all
into the hands of the ones who can travel.

You draw your fears around you like a cloak
You raise your head, take deep breaths,
exhale and
say a silent
prayer of thanks
another day will come
another opportunity
to rise.

YOU are America.
AMERICA is you.

For the New American

The Reunited
(In memory of Dalbert)

Your pain is palpable
it is rock hard.
Silently
it travels with you
as you go out and
as you come in
daily.

Just below the surface it simmers
in the cells,
in the gut
in the blood.
It is your ever present companion
on anniversaries,
birthdays, at weddings
and funerals.

The days and nights
and nights and days
separated the daily bonding.
Spirits occupy the spaces
at the empty tables

in the kitchens, in the churches,
synagogues and mosques . . .

The (un)broken ties
threaded only by
history,
by recollections of old
are stained
on your memory walls.
The hard rock,
the cellular damage
repaired only by
the meeting.
The touch of the flesh
the searching and meeting of eyes
the exchange of breaths
the first hello
of
the reunited.

For the New American

The Undocumented

My life through a mirror
here
hiding in plain sight
there
hiding out of sight
same status,
Underground.

Low profile
lest I am found and
deported
lest I am found and
become the
departed
6 feet
Underground.

Jamaica Calling

How to Listen to Reggae
(Vibing on Bob)

Sit back
Kick up the bass
Level the treble
Meditate and then
Get up and gyrate

Sometimes you might feel you want to get up and groove
    (stand up!)
but if things get a little too fast, you can always cool it down
    (the pace that is)
Another time you might feel that you just have to hold on now
    (to what you have in hand)
don't hold on too tight, let it flow
    (or let it go)

II

Sit back
Kick up the bass
Level the treble
Meditate and then
Get up and gyrate

One day when you are taking it slow,
doing a little levitation (mediation)
in a cottage away from it all
> (in Negril?)
it hits you that this music is fantastic, you decide
> (its electric!)

III

Sit back
Kick up the bass
Level the treble
Meditate and then
Get up and gyrate

Even when the rain *a fall* and the *dutty* tough
the music makes you feel like shouting
> (Jah!)
you tell the bass man to *leggo* the music vibes
> (they'll be *nuttin but* sweetness tonite!)

Jamaica Goodbye

Goodbye my love
I have loved you for a lifetime
I have loved you
from the top down –
    the misty tips of your mountain range and
from the ground up –
    the slippery stones in your river bottom
I have loved you
since the voices of the children echoed
the "sugar and spice and all that's nice"
little girls were made of and
"slugs and snails and puppy dogs tails,
that comprised little boys
my love knew no bounds.

No bounds as we roamed the Parishes, 14,
sentiments, smells and voices rising in song
rising independently in 1962
the ebb and flow of voices
year in, year out.
Then you were
turning 48,

and we turned to unbridled weeping
moaning of love, past and present
moaning of desire
moaning of hunger
moaning of pain

Heal my love, heal
take charge
take charge of your children, your brother, your sister
take charge of your fellow man and woman
exult in the brotherhood and sisterhood of life
exult in the language of the mortals
the language of the immortals
Nanny, Paul, Marcus, Mary, Busta and Lady B,
Sam, Miss Lou, Bob and the Manleys
they, the speakers of the language of love, portrayed love
yuh striving today because of their love
and the love from Jah above

II

Don't delay my love, the decay is imminent,
the decay intolerable,
spewing its wine through the Parishes, 14,
we are masters and participants
in a drunken slide, together holding hands
like children on a journey
crossing a busy street, holding fast together
hoping for safe passage

children crisp, neatly dressed, clean and pure hearted
hopeful, danger unforeseen
now catastrophic, the slippery slope.

Expel the wine
look back my love, before you step forward
your children have grown up walking,
talking, listening, not seeing,
their minds engaged not by thoughts of higher heights
or love of self and others in humility,
nor respect or human engagement

The bondage of the wine
the bondage of your mind, my love, had cast you
to the beginning of a time when you grunted
no language escaped your mouth
for you were barely human
look back, wake up my love
rise
rise
your Blue Mountains are your inspiration
your children cry out
their blood, their human body stands for you
let not a drop of their precious blood be shed in vain

Rise to the occasion
resist
the time has come for you to stand strong
stand straight my love, rise and

we will stand with you
or it is goodbye forever
goodbye, whitewashed stones, bright rainbows,
peacocks in bloom,
sun washed streets
goodbye scents of mangoes robin and number 11,
ripe bananas, tangerines,
sweetsop, codfish cooking on Sunday morning
goodbye morning mists, the salty taste of your flowing water
sights of the bougainvillea, the soft petals of your hibiscus
goodbye wide smiles, hearts beating, human hearts beating
it is goodbye to love
fi now
cause in mi heart of hearts, mi know
yuh soon come forward

III

Yuh mus' come
for wi not leaving you out
We stand with you, my love
we will not let you fall
Lennox will show you the moves and so will
Jody-Ann, Usain and Merlene, Carla and Naomi,
 Shari and Harry and
mother and daughter Clarke, General Colin, Michael,
 Charmaine,
Grace, Oliver and Joan, Diane to name a few

they stood for you, we will stand with you
for "out of many we are one."

The seeds of our past were planted in your blessed ground
You'll soon come back, but it might take a few rounds
our elders took their first breath of your sanctified air
their hearts and minds were formed in your wooden chairs
Oh love, dear love, your love knew no bounds
no bounds as we tarried in your Parishes, 14,
no bounds
as some left with your much needed protein
they left on the tail winds of the Caribbean
carrying Air Jamaica
carrying the black, the green and the gold
they spread it far and wide to
Australia, Ghana, Japan and Germany, with respect to your British and US progeny
all are trying to be like them
all now constrained to honor you with the mighty hyphen

No, we cyaan leave you out lovey
yuh always in the mix
Right now though it seem that you jus' between and betwixt
our ancestors did all for Queen and country
it's for the sake of love we offer you our bounty
So we know yuh coming
the future is in sight
for you taught us well

you taught us right
"the heights that great men reached and kept, were not
    attained by sudden flight"
so we'll toil with you darling, all day and all night
and wi have fait
dat wid massa God mercy
you wi go tru . . .
after you drink up yuh cerasee.

Humor for any Age and Stage

Children are Like Sweets

There are two relationships
that I hold on to
for dear life.
Those with my children
and with sweets

Here's how I feel about both my children and my sweets:

- When I am away from them I miss them,
  I can't wait to see them again.

- Thinking about them makes me smile.
- I sacrificed a lot to get them.
- Sometimes I am embarrassed when I am around them.
- Often I feel that they are controlling me.

Ah, these children and sweets,
We have special times together that make me happy.

But they make me gain weight,
and no matter what they do,
I have a hard time throwing them out.

The doctors can't explain it,
but I know, I am sure, sure, sure,
sure
that they are the culprits,
they are responsible
for giving me
grey hairs.

Humor for Any Age and Stage

How to Take Your Medicine

Take this, anti**inflamm**atory.
    Blessings to you!

And this, blood-**thinner**.
    BAM, BAM, BOOM, BOOM . . . . . .
    wake up, break up, flow through!

In the morning
take the medicine tablet whole
or in pieces.
not the chocolate Reese's pieces

Later in the day
take prunes, metamucil or magnesia
liquid or solid bits,
not the spirits

You can take your medicine
standing, sitting or when you are lying
keep trying,
We don't want you dying

II

At night
break off a finger of ginger
you know you must let it linger
so too with the Leaf of Life
maybe you have to take them twice
roll the dice,
maybe even thrice

Friends will come
when their day is done
they'll bring a little homily,
even a bit of comedy

Take it in
it's not a sin
to grin,
It's not gin

If all else fails,
get the bush tea.
It comes with a guarantee.

Sir Pride

Open your eyes wide
there's an assault on Sir Pride
Sir Pride's had to hide
cause things have gone wild

Take an inspection
the mirror has your reflection
there's hanging, sagging, tightening
it's frightening

During the lecture
a finger made a gesture
and who said that word
that has run amok
even the mother and the child
took a fast duck

We should make some rules
We need some new tools

II

The eyes that meet yours

direct and engaging
are masking the facts
unseen and deranging

When the mouth flies faster
than a mouse on a timer
it's concealing the truth,
like a misspent youth

The show of hands
caught correctly candid
snapped fingers that snatch
all they can catch

We should make some rules
We need some new tools

III

The leg's in a cast
they report to the agent
oh they are determined
breathless, but
cogent

My, but how they walked fast
a sprinter could not pass
bolting through the parking lot
out of sight

and
out of earshot

Sir Pride, I applaud you
look what you've gone through
but
bringing you back
is going to cost you
because . . .

your replacement's paying
a bounty
to keep
you
out of the county

Inspirational

Fight Right

For a comeback
your mind must
wrap around
and
turn 360

then,
bow from waist to toe.
Fling hands high
and
to the ground

lift your knee
count to three.
Run in place
and clench your face
for the race

put one foot before the other
start the walk and the talk.
Ask yourself who can help.

then, take advice from the master
you'll go faster.

The winner knows the way
saves you a day.
Now
you're a
comeback kid
with skid!

Inspirational

Little Treasures

Nation builders are you,
who stay the course
like the glue
that runs
into every nook and cranny,
firmly setting the
foundation,
the building blocks,
just so.

It is not a speed chase,
you don't follow
the rat race,
you just look
into the eyes
of your future prize
and teach them,
to be
wise.

Later, each may become
President, Prime Minister,

commentator,
undertaker.
Shakespeare, Magellan
Garvey or a Garvey-ite.
Everyone is bright,
not just a socialite.

Your contribution
to this great land,
starts with your helping hand.
As parents, we give to you
in trust, our little treasures,
to shape and mold
to expose to thoughts and concepts
and reasoning's sublime.
Take your time.

We know you're giving
good measure
to our little treasures.
You are a nation builder
not an outfielder.
You're in the mix
day to day
you carry the sway.
All the way.

Inspirational

Love

The tonic, the power, the fruit of life
is found in a four letter word
LOVE

The Beatles said that the only thing we need is love.
It's true.
Love offers you benefits that
cannot
be found elsewhere
no matter where you look.

Scientists, psychologists, politicians,
parents, creationists,
evolutionists, believers,
heretics, even derelicts
all come back to this one truth,
love's not just for the youth.

Love gives you everything you need
from when you were a mere seed.
The mother's
protection,

which came from
seduction.
The childhood kiss
that was pure bliss,
mending,
in a heartbeat
the scrapes and the small bleeds.

That youngster who was corrupt
even the one whose was abrupt
made a
turnaround,
when love was
found.

That intractable old codger
will live so much longer
the ointment
is clear
see through,
my dear, it's love.

Great men and women,
you say you are all knowing.
Take LOVE
through the country and see the effects
on the gentry.

It will be quite potent
our society will be

Inspirational

content,
when they receive the
right quotient.
And your cap will get
the feather.
all the better.

So I make a motion
that you include this
bold notion,
in every legislation,
that we pass in our nation.
Longing **O**bjector wants to cast a **V**ote **E**arly
   and often (the LOVE bill)

I guarantee there will be
no fighting for funding,
just
carousing.
All love needs is
foreplay
before it has its day.

Me Hiding

I want to be
Me
I want the power to
Be
I want the knowledge to
free
me
So I can
Be
Me

Inspirational

Rise to the Beat

Rise to the beat
the song stirs within you
whispering

Take the hand of the little ones
connect their minds, hearts, souls and bodies
to be one

Rise to the beat
the ancestors reach
to anoint you
to appoint you
as transmitter
as teacher

Rise to the beat
one by one
one on one
take it now
pass it on

Feel the drumbeat

Sow Stones, Reap Daffodils?

Ah,
It's agony
I can't stand to watch
waiting for them to hatch.
The tiny yellow of their feathers
peeks out
as the shell membrane cracks

The webbed feet
take a tentative
tipsy, toes-y touch,
as she tries to right herself
Ungainly,
Teetering.
A .... h ...
she's got it
step into
the world.

The birth of a chick
through
the diaphanous bonds

Inspirational

of the membrane
enveloping her

I breathe,
relieved.
My chick is my child.
I, the mother fowl
We reap
nothing other
than
what we sow.

Taboo, Thank You

It's not taboo
To say thank you.
I can say it to you
"Thank you."

There is no law to rue
or a speech snafu.
Just a heart to heart
"Thank you"
for all that you do.

And
don't you dare say
"Shoo, its nothing, Boo."
I know you.

Inspirational

Wind Catcher

Run with the wind . . .
it's languid
on a clear day,
boisterous
like a skirt chaser,
on a cloudy day

Catch it
in the hand.
Bounce it
with your hip,
taste it
with your lip

Throw
your head back.
Let it embrace you
side to side,
enjoy
the glide.

Social Commentary

A Word to the Faithful

My Dear:

Is it old fashioned, dare I say "old school," to have faith?
The scriptures say, "... **faith** is the substance of things hoped for, the evidence of things not seen."
Can **faith** move mountains?
Can bare **faith** really move the Blue Mountains?

I believe that we truly must have **faith**.
We demonstrate this **faith** each and every day when we send our children to school
check into a hotel
go to the hospital
undergo surgery
eat out at a restaurant
climb a mountain
drive a car
ride in a car
cross a busy street
step into an elevator
fly in an airplane
get up each day and walk outside of our home ...

We may not view our actions as a "demonstration of faith"
as we may abhor even the mere whisper of a connection
with the word spirituality or the word religion.
But these words do not necessarily connote
faith in an Almighty.

The word **faith**, in fact, can be interpreted
as a mere expression of our trust in each other.
Or just a hope that we will be treated by others,
the way we would treat them,
if the occasion demands it.

So you do not have to call it **faith**.
Call it what you will.
Just allow me to use that word loosely.

In closing, I encourage and applaud your hope,
I applaud your trust in and deep regard for your fellow
man and woman.
Your **faith** in them gets you through the day.
Your **faith** in them lifts your spirits, not your blood pressure
and each time you see people less fortunate,
empathize with them.
Their **faith** guides them to hope for a better day.
"There, but for the grace of God go [you and] I."

Social Commentary

Designed for Extinction

We keep hearing that
to live longer we need to
cut out fat (*eat right*) and
keep our cells humming,
maybe with a little drumming (*exercise our bodies*)
and a bit of
mulling (*exercise our minds*).

But,
every day
we see an invention
that has no relation to that
convention.

These days, that dinner plate
has no weight
just a few nibblets
and
tablets
that look like
gadgets.

That new telephone
keeps you connected,
all alone
in your home.
It is a zone
that does not
let you roam.

That new Nook
is not a book,
tactile
and
arresting,
which begs for
digressing.

I fear that these new inventions
designed with
good intentions
will take our bodies
to the
brink
of extinction.

But
before you can blink
this new kind of think
may cause Chanel
to create

Social Commentary

a
panel.

They'll call in
Armani's army,
the Boeing makers
the decorators and
of course their drapers.

Rolex and Bulova
may jump into the
brouhaha,
saying
"It's cruel,
what will we do
with
our jewels."

Coach sent them a bag
made with the
American flag.
Wedgewood
broke the ice with them,
twice.
That was
nice.

Give the inventors
their due
they are astute.

They turned their
hobby
into a
lobby.

Their ideas
they've inked
with the legislators'
wink,
so
they do not fear their inventions will
sink.

Social Commentary

÷ Divide and Conquer

This is often
used
by those
who choose
to abuse.

They often rally
to increase their tally
they aim to
✕ multiply
exponentially.

Isn't it folly
to have a full trolley
when the extra, super, and ultra portions
create a ✚ plus size girth
that hurts.

Your clout may lead to a revolt
your favor may be out
as the labor have learnt
to add, divide, subtract and multiply.

oh,
you sigh.

why not — subtract all that ill will?
consider taking a chill pill
blame it on the desire
to see the nation
go higher.

÷ divide the spoils
not the labor
Make it all add up and be = equal
or they're liable
to get legal.

Social Commentary

Fringe (foods, language, schools, friends) Rule

Let's start with food.
Through the ages we've been told
that the foods we need to sustain life
are carbs, protein, fruits and vegetables (CPFV);
this teaching is centuries old.

Lately, I've have a hard time
identifying
these CPFVfoods
when I drop in to do
my shopping.

It is mystifying—
I am really trying
to find out if the new foods
are CPFVs
that have just been retooled for
21st century moods (fools).

They come in a variety of forms;
some are liquid, some are solid,

and still others
are something in between

Soon the stores will have a separate isle
with a sign that says "REAL food here"
The shoppers who enter there
will be those who admit
they cannot read
small print
nor
three or four syllable words such as
genetically modified,
synthetic,
monosodium glutamate
and other new food terms.

II

I also have issues with LANGUAGE
lately everything is described as HYPERbole
or dropped casually
supposedly to charm
but calculated to harm
It's like they are saying
nibble on that
you goat
while they're delivering a
wretched
footnote,

which must be
"politically correct" or
"no offense intended"
—splendid!

Sometimes you hear "Not that I'm a—," or
"to be politically correct . . ."
you fill in the blank.
The KISS method is so refreshing,
it may need arresting
Keep
    It
        Simple
            Stupid
just KISS me and I'll return
the favor!

III

Even with SCHOOLS.
Should I CHARTER or will the child
further falter?
Go ONLINE to spare the time?
How about a MAGNET
although it sounds like
a
dragnet
Ok, let's get this together. Line them up
side by side,

compare
good, better, best
Let's put them to the test.

IV

Most of all with FRIENDS.
I am confused
about
whom I should LIKE and whom I should
not.
Help me choose, "Youse."

We've come to a day
when fringe is ok.

Social Commentary

Letter to the Upsetters
(The Banned Books Crusaders)

Pardon me for writing
I try not to be trifling
I have a genuine issue
break out your tissue

After you read this
I hope you'll agree
it is not much ado about nothing,
it's something

Read it carefully
don't worry about the length
its not the
Magna Carta I sent

It's not a tell all
I'm not revealing any secrets
It's not "the scarlet letter,"
it's better

It may move you
to cry
or sigh

soon you'll learn why

It may break some ranks
there will be no thanks
it's like the Pentagon Papers,
there will be no takers

After you read it
tell others
RELEASE it
don't
ban
my pronouncements
you know they are
not nonsense.

Social Commentary

More Laws, Less Happiness

Seven continents broad
the earth,
contained within and
bound by water.

Can't run, can't walk, can't hide
laws find you inside
and outside.
In the dark night
in the park in daylight
and not just in the boardroom,
in the bedroom.

Can't cry, can't fly, can't die
laws find you eating
and drinking.
Don't let them find you thinking.
In a hot air balloon
and not just in the womb,
in the tomb.

Every day they trail you, coming closer
catching up to you
"Boo."

II

Send them packing
to the loo or
to the zoo
let them catch
the flu

let you and me talk
let you and me listen
let you and me laugh
let you and me dance
meditate
create
and mediate

Boo
Shoo
We have life to do.

Social Commentary

News

Morning news
evening news
I have such a short fuse

You can even watch the babble
on cable,
if you are able

It's the 24 hour blues
the news,
Views about loose screws.

Listening to the newscaster
reporting on the London terrorist attack – July 2005
Newscaster: "Terrorists strike London"
Child: "But . . . London is not a person!!!"

OxyMoron

Valpac
This means you are getting
something for the lowest price.
Break it down.
"Val" means value, valuable, maybe even
priceless.
Would I part with my value(able)s?
You try to get them away from me
and see

"Pac" means a group of things
placed together in one container
glued, bound, inseparable.
so my value(able)s, prizes and possessions, that makes me
me . . .
is
bargain priced
$1 per pack?

A fad
or
just sad?

Social Commentary

Politricks = Politics

INSTRUCTIONS: Read the phrases in the order of their numbers.

    Poli[tics]tricks
          is
              the (**.1**)
Uncomfortble (**.2**)
Zipping of your lips lest you (**.3**)
Zany (**.5**)
Libelous language (**.7**)
Explode into (**.4**)
Raucous (**.6**)

1.2.3.4.5.6.7

Musing Aloud, Allowed

The Devil's in the Details

The devil's in the details
so *they* say.
keeps me
wondering
if it's an excuse
for more distraction
and inaction.

They are showing themselves up
they have no starch
in their makeup
unlike their forebears
who were committed
and would not
be outwitted.

They had the thirst,
the drive
to fix
whatever they felt
was not realistic.

So came the conventions
of Geneva,
So came the treaties
of Rome,
So came the declarations,
charters, regulations,
and more.
I can't keep score!

Suffice it to say
your elders had their way
with grit and spunk
talk
became a call to
action.
They sure made some
traction.

Your task is no less remarkable
don't sweat it
with parables
put shoulders to the wheel
pedal to the metal
and the proverbial
nose to the grindstone.
Break through that rock
turn back the clock.

The Romans built Rome
the Greeks built Greece
both fell
we both know quite well
it was
that devil
from
Hell.

Your future is much greater
now you know that
he's a hater.
Here's the tip, get a grip
Don't look
in your coattails
he'll be hiding
in the details.

When you find him,
apprise him
that
this time,
his Hell won't be
rising
through
his
conniving.

Social Commentary

The Skin I'm In

God, let me win
against the skin I'm in.
Audacious
I can't cover,
alter or remove it,
irreverent
it goes before me
announcing,
"I'm in!"

It has its detractors
the lock steppers,
patient marshals destined for general
who protest
with precision,
"She can't come in!"

But precious
precocious
stands forward in time,
at the finish line.

Brash
sometimes hesitant
but still expectant,
like a child
or a blushing bride.

The compulsion
to BE,
that bratty she
whispers constantly,
she's the key to me.
Sometimes
she heralds with bagpipes
mockingly,
with glee.

She reigns supreme
in the glow of the snow
she'll not part company
like the sun for the moon,
accommodatingly.
She will not subside
when the tide retires,
she'll come with me
to my destiny.

This living skin
I bring with me
journeys from inside

to outside.
Our paths collide.
That spark is a feeling
that leaves me reeling,
but I'm in control
I am feeling
I insist,
"I'm in control,"
as I'm kneeling,
but she's not
believing.

Travel Ban

"Excuse me, I have to search you."
"Sure," I gestured to the bag on the table
Eyes, firm, stared at me fixedly.
I took two steps back, "Do you mean search my person?"
a firm nod in response.
I looked behind and around me, perplexed, slowly digesting
"Are you sure?"
Another firm nod,
"Why?"
Silence
"There must be some mistake, ask someone in charge, your supervisor."
"Ma'am, we have to search everyone."
"You mean to tell me you search every single traveler who comes through there?" my eyes and hand swept the
    entrance
"Yes, Maam"
"What could I have done to avoid this?"
"Nothing."
Tense moments(the flight is waiting, my life is on the other side)
"All right."

Social Commentary

Submission.
Spit forms, choking.
Repulsed.
Why bother with a travel ban?

Musing Aloud

Call to Order

Call to order
Yes, you too, Brother
Love that tam
brimming,
preventing the hair from going on the lam

What's that you say?
Was that a pitch for the Smithsonian?
Ah, you're a historian . . . .
We'll take that under advisement,
as long as there's no self aggrandizement

Call to order
Yes, Mommy? Where's Tommy?
Your son, it's time he signed in
He went hang-gliding? Who'll chide him?
You'd better dial him, or I'll fine him

Call to order
First off, the limit on talking
will be strictly enforced

Second, no activity, except for mouth gravity
If you can't agree, we will still remain crime-free
we have a policeman, who says he's a Christian
So either way, we will have our say
twin forces in one man, the spirit and the physical

Third on the agenda, is surrender.
Last time we gave them the egg
now it looks like they want the goose
the entire caboose
talk time, then vote.
But before you make your imprint,
hear me distinct,
once we give it
we are extinct.

Musing Aloud

Creative Writing 101

Uu Uoooh
it's a
haiku.

Before that it was a
sonnet
that gave me a bee in my
bonnet

Could I say
I had a flu
or am I making much ado?

I wonder if Miss Lou
would say,
"Pu hoo hoo
lady do
get to work
rhyming, counting lines
bending, stretching the mind
go through,
advance

serendipity will create the nuance
arriving softly in the night,
so you can rise to write at daylight."

I'll begin at the beginning, I need to master this craft.
I
AM
Bold,
Interested,
and
Courageous;
pass me that
PEN

-Ta-

start the
METER.

*Louise Bennett, Jamaican writer, poet, folklorist, and educator

Crosses to Bear

He's too debonair, but with a flair	The temple teachings, I swear:
"Your aura has the power"	"give a testimony or give me money"
I cower.	It's not funny.
Fighting the revolution, I can bear	(Pre)conversation conclusions. Beware.
"more weapons, more (wo)men, let's overpower them"	"talking heads, deeply conflicted: their journals, fragmented and restricting"
We need friends.	Why can't they be pointed?

Father's Day is Every Day

Father's Day is every day
because you are
a father,
every day.

You cannot pass on the post
of teaching a child today;
from such a job,
there is no holiday.

They came here, made by you,
that sweet girl or boy,
causing you to
work, sing and smile, play, pay, pray and
make excuses for their delay.

They are the center of life
You, the coach, is on the outside,
deciding when to yell, do a sit down,
or run with them,
to show them how it's done.

Musing Aloud

All in all, at the end of the day,
you must know that there is no other way
to raise that that boy or girl
no other way in the whole wide world.

Happy Father's Day!

Genius

Boy you're a Genius
            E
            N
            I
            U
            S
you had a bit of help
from the two of us

the GENe that you got from me
was improved with the one from he
Zen
we
became thee

It all started with
I
and he.
We're to blame
if you're inflamed
just
US

Gifting

Nothing today
nothing for the last 30
call #1: can you do . . . .
taking
call #2: can you do . . .
taking
call #3: ah begging you to do . . .

All without a proper thank you
For you, its
nothing new

Let me set the record straight
I was taught
it is better to give than to receive
this is even in the Bible.
so why don't people follow its teachings?

gifting makes you feel good
it makes the receiver feel even better
who needs a psy-cho-lo-gist
when a gift has an echo
that spreads
and lasts longer, than the words of an apologist

Musing Aloud, Allowed

I was taught
when you give, give the best you have
my grandmother said that
so why don't people listen to their elders.

gifting makes you feel good
it makes the receiver feel even better
who needs a psy-cho-lo-gist
when a gift has an echo
that spreads
and lasts longer, than the words of an apologist?

I was taught
"do unto others as you would have them do unto you"
the Bible, my grandmother . . . stop there
really, who would have a problem with that, dear?

gifting makes you feel good
it makes the receiver feel even better
who needs a psy-cho-lo-gist
when a gift has an echo
that spreads
and lasts longer, than the words of an apologist?

I learned lately
when you give, give what you know the other person
would want to receive
someone from the "me generation" told me that
that's phat!

Musing Aloud

I am Willing

I have to be
still
to hear the
Will (of God)
so that I can
distill and fulfill,
till I can no longer
climb the
Hill.

I have the drill
and now have perfected my
skill
I will do my part to
impart from the heart,
and before I depart
I will
make my
Will

Musing Aloud, Allowed

More Than Just a Number

Whoever said "age is just a number" is right,
Why do we stop telling the AGE after 40?
Before that double digit,
We thought we were IT,
we thought we were with it,
so we proudly and loudly announced it.
Then 40 crept up and we wanted the buck to
stop there.

I predict
in fact, we need an edict
that restores age as the indicator,
the incubator,
of fulsome wisdom.
This way, AGE will
give us freedom,
it will be like a getaway or a tax holiday

Some have said AGE
is a STAGE.
I find that StAGggEring.
Are they trying to be flattering,
or are they just pandering,
since they know that with each second that passes,
we are AGEing,
not staging?

II

The more pressing concern is the
enlargement of the number factory
Pretty soon, you will not need your birth certificate
to prove who you are
You will just need to provide a number.
Then, I'll join the ranks of the
fumblers, who silently abhor
their proliferation, considering how to
do away with the number factory trajectory

Here is how it adds up:
Even before you took your first breath,
a number was reserved for you.
You life ends, you are assigned one
in between, the numbers pile
a mile high
student identification
social security

contact
credit card
citation
passenger
passport
password
phone
account
arrest
alien
detainee
employee
national identification
juror . . .

You say,
"My name is _____"
          your name goes here

The dratted response,
"I need your username and password to complete your transaction."
"Uh, Uh, let's see . . . let me find it . . . give me a minute . . . maybe two."

Musing Aloud

Small Talk Just got Smaller

K?
    Yea
    U?

Oui (French = yes)
Brie?
    Sí (Spanish = yes)

Translation:
How are you doing? I would love to catch up with you for a meal. When are you available?

    I'm alright, yes, tonight works for me.

Snap, Pop and Pour

"Snap!"
The sound was
like a heart attack.

"Crackle, pop!"
Frizzy froth,
spilling helplessly,
on a hippity hop.

With voices drowning in laughter
it could not falter.
Every reason was a season
or a truce
to get loose with the juice.

Now it's the end of the sing-a-long
what went wrong?
Now there are just tears on a rainbow
floating like a sideshow.
And now I know
It's because you told him
to go.

Musing Aloud

The Point of Ranting

Irre-verent is not the same as irre-Levant!
The letter that defines their difference
takes a pose,
not in repose,
it's a vertical stance
of resistance

When you want to act outside
of the expected,
seeking to normalize what
some would consider to be
abhorrent or offensive,
the behavior is called irreverent

To some,
it causes a great deal of ire,
when you conspire, to
flaunt and strut
your stuff,
without being rebuffed.

But, you had to don that stubborn hat

to stand (and you sometimes sat),
for hours on end
to defend
your right,
to your existence.
Your vertical
resistance
took you the distance

Immanuel Kant might have found you to be
decadent,
a
vanguard, or
avant-garde.
No, Kant would not find you
irre-verent or
irre-Levant.
Go, rant!

Musing Aloud

Tone Deaf

"Do you have something to say?"
A rhetorical question.
at age seventeen she hates it when I ask.
My tone tells her that
this conversation is over.

At age eight she had
tried hard to
teach me

"Mom, I don't mean any disrespect or anything,
but your tone,
it drives me crazy – I mean . . .
ah, you have other tones that I like better,
when you are being nice,
but then you have these tones
like *sartastic
you really have to cancel these tones
from your tone list, Mom."

But I am tone deaf!

*this is the child's pronunciation

About the Author

Sherna Spencer's roots spring from the Island of Jamaica. Her love of books and language began there in a Parish library, in Manchester. After moving to the U.S., she attended Le Moyne College in upstate New York. There, she obtained a Bachelors degree, with dual majors in English and Spanish. She continued her studies in Italy and thereafter completed her law degree at the University of Miami School of Law. She is currently an attorney in Fort Lauderdale, Florida. For nine years, she was the host of a live radio program centering on issues relating to immigration and nationality law-the program is broadcast to listeners in South Florida and the Bahamas.

www.ingramcontent.com/pod-product-compliance
Lightning Source LLC
Chambersburg PA
CBHW020659300426
44112CB00007B/443